LIFE AND HEALTH
INSURANCE GUIDE

Understanding Policies: Simplifying Insurance Decisions,
Benefits, Protecting Loved Ones, Secure your Future,
Financial Peace, Smart Choices and Medical Solutions

George Leo

DEDICATION

To those seeking security and peace of mind, this book is
dedicated to you. May it bring clarity, confidence, and hope
as you protect what matters most—your loved ones and
future. Thank you to my family, whose support inspires every
page, and to the readers, who make this effort worthwhile.

TABLE OF CONTENTS

George Leo

ACKNOWLEDGMENTS

I deeply thank my family for their unwavering encouragement and patience throughout this process. To the experts and professionals who generously shared their insights, your guidance was invaluable. To my readers, your trust fuels this effort. This book exists because of the support, love, and belief of those around me.

INTRODUCTION

Life and health insurance are not just policies; they are commitments to protecting what matters most—your well-being and the future of those you care about. At times, the complexities surrounding insurance can feel overwhelming, making it hard to know where to start or how to choose the right options. This guide aims to simplify the process, offering clear, practical advice to help you make informed decisions. Whether it's ensuring that your family is financially secure or covering unexpected medical expenses, understanding these policies can bring peace of mind and financial stability. By addressing common questions, shedding light on important considerations, and outlining actionable steps, this guide provides the support you need to maximize the value of your life and health insurance. Let's focus on empowering you to protect your future with confidence and care.

CHAPTER 1

UNDERSTANDING INSURANCE BASICS

1.1 What is Life and Health Insurance?

Life and health insurance are protective measures designed to offer financial security in times of uncertainty. Life insurance provides monetary support to beneficiaries upon the death of the insured, ensuring that loved ones are not left grappling with financial burdens during an already difficult time. Health insurance, on the other hand, is structured to cover medical expenses, reducing the out-of-pocket costs associated with doctor visits, hospital stays, surgeries, and prescriptions. These types of insurance are not just products; they represent a safety net woven with the threads of preparation and compassion for oneself and one's family.

Life and health insurance fundamentally provide comfort and a sense of stability. While no one can predict when illness or death might affect them, these policies stand as a testament to responsibility and forward-thinking. They offer a sense of control amid the uncontrollable, ensuring that those who depend on you are protected even when you can't be there to offer direct support.

1.2 The Purpose and Importance of Insurance

The core purpose of insurance lies in mitigating risk and ensuring stability. Life and health insurance, specifically, play critical roles in protecting an individual's financial health and safeguarding their family's future. For instance, imagine a situation where the primary earner of a household unexpectedly passes away. Without life insurance, the family may struggle to cover mortgage payments, utility bills, or education costs. The emotional toll of such a loss is immense, and adding financial strain only magnifies the challenges faced by surviving family members.

Health insurance serves a similar protective role. In the absence of adequate health coverage, a sudden medical emergency can drain savings or plunge a family into debt. Medical procedures, especially those requiring specialized care or hospitalization, come with substantial costs. Health insurance helps absorb these expenses, allowing individuals to seek necessary treatments without the fear of financial ruin. It turns what could be overwhelming situations into ones that feel more controllable. Life and health insurance hold value that goes beyond personal benefits. On a larger scale, these forms of insurance contribute to economic stability by ensuring that medical costs and loss of income do not cascade into wider financial crises for families and communities.

1.3 Key Terminology Explained

Understanding insurance can feel overwhelming without clarity on the key terms involved. Here are explanations for some fundamental terms:

- **Premium:** This is the amount paid, often monthly or annually, to maintain an insurance policy. Think of it as the cost of keeping your safety net active.
- **Beneficiary:** The person or persons designated to receive the payout from a life insurance policy when the insured passes away. This individual could be a spouse, child, or any person chosen by the policyholder.
- **Deductible:** In health insurance, this is the portion the policyholder must pay on their own before the insurance begins covering costs. For instance, if your deductible is $1,000, you must spend that amount on

approved medical services before your insurance contributes.

- **Coverage:** The specific benefits and services that an insurance policy agrees to pay for. It outlines what is included (e.g., doctor visits, surgery, prescriptions) and often what is not.

- **Policyholder:** The individual who holds the insurance policy and is covered by its benefits.

- **Claim:** A request submitted to an insurance company for payment according to the policy's terms. For example, if you have health insurance and undergo surgery, your medical provider will submit a claim for payment.

- **Term Life Insurance:** A life insurance policy that offers coverage for a set timeframe, such as 10, 20, or 30 years. If the insured passes away during the term, the beneficiary receives the policy's death benefit.

- **Whole Life Insurance:** A type of permanent life insurance that stays active as long as premiums are paid. It provides not only a death benefit but also a savings component, accumulating cash value over time. Familiarity with these terms empowers individuals to make more informed decisions when selecting a policy that aligns with their needs and priorities.

1.4 How Insurance Policies Work

Insurance policies operate based on a contract between the policyholder and the insurer. This contract outlines the terms, conditions, and extent of coverage provided. Here's a straightforward breakdown of how these policies function:

1. **Application and Underwriting:** The process begins when an individual applies for insurance. The insurer evaluates various factors such as age, health status, occupation, and lifestyle to determine eligibility and set the premium. This evaluation is known as underwriting. For example, a young, non-smoking individual with no pre-existing conditions will likely have lower premiums compared to an older individual with health concerns.

2. **Premium Payments:** Once the policy is active, the policyholder must pay premiums regularly to maintain coverage. The amount of the premium is influenced by the level of risk associated with insuring the individual. Missing payments can lead to policy termination, which can mean losing coverage altogether.

3. **Policy Activation and Benefits:** For life insurance, once activated, the policy guarantees that a sum will be paid to the beneficiary upon the death of the insured, as long as premiums are up to date. Health insurance, by contrast, provides benefits as needed—whether it's routine check-ups or emergency care. Policyholders usually present their insurance information at the time of service, after which claims are submitted for processing.

4. **Claims Process:** For life insurance, claims are typically initiated by the beneficiary after the policyholder's death. The insurance company then reviews the claim, verifies the policy's terms, and issues the payout. In health insurance, claims are often handled by healthcare providers who submit them directly to the insurer. The policyholder might need to provide additional information or proof of service, depending on the terms.

5. **Payouts and Coverage Limits:** Life insurance policies offer a one-time payout to the beneficiary, which can be used at their discretion. Health insurance policies come with annual or lifetime coverage limits, meaning there is a cap on the amount the insurer will pay over a certain period. Exceeding these limits means the policyholder is responsible for any additional expenses.

CHAPTER 2

TYPES OF LIFE INSURANCE

Selecting a life insurance policy can be overwhelming with the range of options available. Understanding what each type offers helps make an informed choice that aligns with one's needs and those of their loved ones. Here, we break down the primary types of life insurance and their unique characteristics to simplify the process.

2.1 Term Life Insurance

Term life insurance is usually the easiest and most budget-friendly option. It provides protection for a set period, usually lasting from 10 to 30 years. If the policyholder passes away during this term, the beneficiaries receive a payout known as the death benefit. One of the main advantages of term life insurance is its affordability compared to other types, making it a suitable choice for young families or individuals who need coverage for a particular financial need, such as paying off a mortgage or funding a child's education. However, term life insurance has a finite duration. Once the policy term ends, there is no payout, and coverage stops unless renewed or converted to a permanent policy. This temporary nature may be seen as a drawback for those seeking lifelong coverage. Still, term life insurance continues to be a favored choice because of its straightforwardness and cost-effectiveness.

2.2 Whole Life Insurance

Whole life insurance stands out for its lifelong coverage and additional financial benefits. Whole life insurance, unlike term policies, remains active for a lifetime, provided premiums are consistently paid. The policy accumulates cash value over time, which can be borrowed or withdrawn when necessary. This cash value component grows at a guaranteed rate and provides a level of financial security that term policies do not offer.

The death benefit is assured, providing peace of mind that loved ones will be taken care of, no matter when the policyholder passes. This certainty comes at a price; whole life insurance premiums are significantly higher than term life insurance. The predictability and added cash value make whole life insurance attractive to those who view insurance as both a protective and investment tool.

2.3 Universal Life Insurance

Universal life insurance gives a greater flexibility than whole life policies. With universal life insurance, the policyholder has the option to adjust their premium payments and death benefit as their financial situation changes over time. This adaptability is a significant advantage for those who want their policy to evolve with their needs.

Similar to whole life insurance, universal life policies also accumulate cash value as time goes on. The growth of this cash value depends on market interest rates and the performance of the insurer's portfolio, which can lead to fluctuations. This variability means that the cash value may not always grow at a predictable rate, adding an element of uncertainty.

One appealing aspect of universal life insurance is the ability to use accumulated cash value to cover premiums after a certain period. This feature can be particularly helpful during times of financial difficulty, providing some breathing room without losing coverage. However, the complexities associated with managing and monitoring the policy's growth can be overwhelming for some. Ensuring the policy stays funded adequately requires attention and possibly adjustments, so it's essential for policyholders to review their policy regularly with their insurer.

2.4 Variable Life Insurance

Variable life insurance merges life coverage with investment options, allowing policyholders to allocate funds to various investment accounts, potentially growing cash value over time. This type of policy allows the policyholder to invest the cash value into various sub-accounts, similar to mutual funds, offering the potential for substantial growth. The death benefit and cash value depend on how well these investments perform, which can lead to greater rewards or significant risks.

For those with a higher risk tolerance and a keen interest in investment, variable life insurance offers a way to potentially increase the policy's value. However, if investments underperform, the cash value and, to some extent, the death benefit may decrease. This variability adds a layer of complexity and requires careful consideration and management. Policyholders must be comfortable with market fluctuations and be willing to take on the responsibility of overseeing their investments.

While variable life insurance can yield high returns, it is not without its pitfalls. For individuals with this policy, the policyholder can invest the cash value in different sub-accounts, similar to mutual funds, providing an opportunity for considerable growth who prefer guaranteed growth and stability, this type of policy may not be the best choice. It's important to balance the desire for investment gains with the need for financial security for loved ones.

2.5 Choosing the Right Life Insurance for Your Needs

Deciding on the most suitable life insurance policy involves assessing one's financial goals, family needs, and risk tolerance. Each type of life insurance serves a distinct purpose, and what works best depends on individual circumstances.

1. Assess Your Financial Situation: Start by reviewing

current and anticipated financial obligations. If coverage is needed for a limited period, such as paying off a mortgage or funding college tuition, term life insurance might be the most practical and cost-effective choice. For those seeking a policy that provides lifelong coverage and an investment component, whole life or universal life insurance could be beneficial.

2. Consider Long-Term Goals: Whole life and universal life insurance are ideal for those who want more than just a death benefit. The added feature of cash value accumulation can provide future financial security, offering a cushion that can be tapped into for emergencies or retirement.

3. Evaluate Risk Tolerance: If the idea of tying cash value growth to market performance seems appealing, variable life insurance might be worth exploring. However, keep in mind the risks associated with potential market downturns. For those who prioritize stability, whole life insurance's guaranteed cash value growth or universal life insurance's flexibility may be better suited.

4. Balance Cost and Benefit: Budget plays a significant role in the decision-making process. Term life insurance typically offers higher coverage amounts for lower premiums, which is valuable for individuals on a tight budget. On the other hand, permanent policies, while more expensive, provide long-term value through death benefits and cash value growth.

5. Future Adaptability: Life is unpredictable, and needs can shift over time. Universal life insurance offers adaptability, enabling policyholders to adjust premium payments and coverage levels to suit their changing needs. This flexibility can be a lifesaver when financial circumstances change, such as during a job loss or an increase in family expenses.

.

CHAPTER 3

TYPES OF HEALTH INSURANCE

Health insurance serves as a crucial tool in managing healthcare expenses and ensuring access to essential medical services. Understanding the various types of health insurance options can make a significant difference in finding the most suitable coverage for individual or family needs. Here, we break down the primary types of health insurance and their unique characteristics to aid in making informed decisions.

3.1 Individual Health Insurance Plans

Individual health insurance plans are policies purchased directly by an individual rather than through an employer or group. These plans offer a variety of coverage options tailored to personal healthcare requirements and budgetary constraints.

One of the key benefits of individual plans is the flexibility they provide. Individuals can choose the level of coverage that best suits their needs, whether it's basic coverage for doctor visits and preventive care or more comprehensive plans that include specialized treatments and hospitalization. These plans typically come in different tiers—such as Bronze, Silver, Gold, and Platinum—each offering varied levels of coverage and out-of-pocket costs.

Purchasing an individual plan often requires careful comparison of premiums, deductibles, co-pays, and the provider network. The premium is the regular payment made to maintain the insurance coverage, while the deductible is the initial amount the insured must pay out-of-pocket before the insurance starts covering specific expenses. High-deductible health plans (HDHPs) paired with Health Savings Accounts (HSAs) can be an appealing option for those who prefer lower monthly premiums and the opportunity to save pre-tax dollars for medical expenses.

3.2 Employer-Sponsored Health Insurance

Employer sponsored health insurance is a type of coverage offered by employers, included as part of an employee benefits package. This type of insurance is one of the most common forms of health coverage in the United States and is typically offered at a reduced premium compared to individual plans.

Employers often shoulder a substantial portion of the premium, easing the financial burden on employees and making the coverage more accessible. These plans may include additional benefits, such as dental and vision coverage, wellness programs, and access to a broader network of healthcare providers. Employees can choose from different plan types, such as Health Maintenance Organizations (HMOs), Preferred Provider Organizations (PPOs), Exclusive Provider Organizations (EPOs), or Point-of-Service (POS) plans.

One of the main advantages of employer-sponsored plans is the shared cost, which reduces the financial burden on employees. Additionally, these plans often include dependent coverage options; ensuring family members can also receive medical benefits. However, employees may have limited choices when it comes to plan selection and must adhere to the employer's chosen insurance provider.

3.3 Government Health Programs (Medicare, Medicaid, CHIP)

Government health programs are public insurance options funded and regulated by federal or state governments to provide essential health coverage to specific groups of people.

Medicare: This program is primarily for individuals aged 65 or older, as well as younger people with certain disabilities or medical conditions. Medicare is divided into parts:

- **Part A (Hospital Insurance):** provides coverage for essential medical services, including inpatient hospital stays, care in skilled nursing facilities, hospice care, and certain home health services.
- **Part B (Medical Insurance):** Covers outpatient care, doctor visits, preventive services, and specific medical supplies necessary for treatment.

- **Part C (Medicare Advantage)**: Offers an alternative to Original Medicare (Parts A and B) through private insurers that include additional benefits, such as dental and vision care.

Part D (Prescription Drug Coverage): Is designed to help reduce the cost of prescription medications, ensuring individuals have access to the treatments they need without excessive financial burden.

Medicaid: A program designed for individuals and families with limited income and resources. It offers comprehensive coverage, including doctor visits, hospital stays, long-term care, and more. Medicaid eligibility and benefits vary by state, as states have the flexibility to tailor their programs to meet local needs. The federal government sets broad guidelines, but states determine specific coverage options and eligibility criteria.

The Children's Health Insurance Program (CHIP) provides vital healthcare coverage for children in families who earn too much to qualify for Medicaid but not enough to afford private insurance. This program ensures that children have access to vital health services, including routine checkups, immunizations, and emergency care.

3.4 Short-Term and Catastrophic Health Insurance

Short-term and catastrophic health insurance plans are designed for specific situations where standard insurance might not be accessible or necessary.

Short-Term Health Insurance: These plans provide temporary coverage, typically lasting from a few months up to a year. They are ideal for individuals in transition—such as between jobs, recent graduates, or those waiting for other coverage to begin. While short-term plans are more affordable than standard plans, they often come with significant limitations, such as excluding pre-existing conditions, limited preventive care, and higher out-of-pocket costs. It's crucial to thoroughly review the policy details to fully understand the coverage provided and any exclusions that may apply.

Catastrophic Health Insurance: Designed primarily for individuals under 30 or those eligible for a hardship or affordability exemption, this insurance offers a safety net for unexpected major medical expenses. While catastrophic plans feature low monthly premiums, they come with significantly high deductibles, making them suitable for young, healthy individuals seeking minimal coverage for worst-case scenarios. These plans are designed to protect against worst-case scenarios—serious illnesses or injuries that could result in substantial medical expenses. They cover essential health benefits and preventive services but require the insured to pay most healthcare costs out-of-pocket until the deductible is met.

Catastrophic plans are a safety net for those who want minimal monthly payments and are willing to take on the financial risk of covering minor medical needs themselves. It's a practical choice for those who do not anticipate frequent medical care but want protection against major unforeseen expenses.

3.5 Supplemental Health Insurance Options

Supplemental health insurance offers extra protection by covering expenses that may not be fully paid by your primary health insurance. These options can be beneficial for individuals who want to enhance their existing coverage and protect themselves against specific medical or financial risks.

Types of Supplemental Insurance Include:

- **Dental and Vision Insurance**: Often not included in basic health plans, these policies help cover routine and emergency dental or eye care.

- **Critical Illness Insurance**: Provides a lump-sum payment if diagnosed with severe conditions such as cancer, heart attack, or stroke. This payment can be used for medical bills, household expenses, or any other needs during treatment.

- **Accident Insurance**: Offers financial assistance in case of injuries resulting from accidents. This can cover hospital stays, medical treatments, and rehabilitation costs.

- **Hospital Indemnity Insurance**: Pays a set amount for each day spent in the hospital, providing financial relief for unexpected hospitalization costs.

Supplemental plans are tailored to bridge gaps in coverage and offer peace of mind by ensuring more complete financial protection. Depending on the nature of the supplemental policy, benefits may come in the form of direct payments or reimbursements that can be used for any purpose, giving policyholders greater flexibility in managing their healthcare expenses.

Finally, navigating the world of health insurance can feel complex, but understanding these key types of coverage helps in making choices that align with one's health and financial needs. Whether choosing individual plans, relying on employer-sponsored benefits, or exploring government programs, each type of insurance brings unique advantages and considerations to ensure comprehensive and practical coverage.

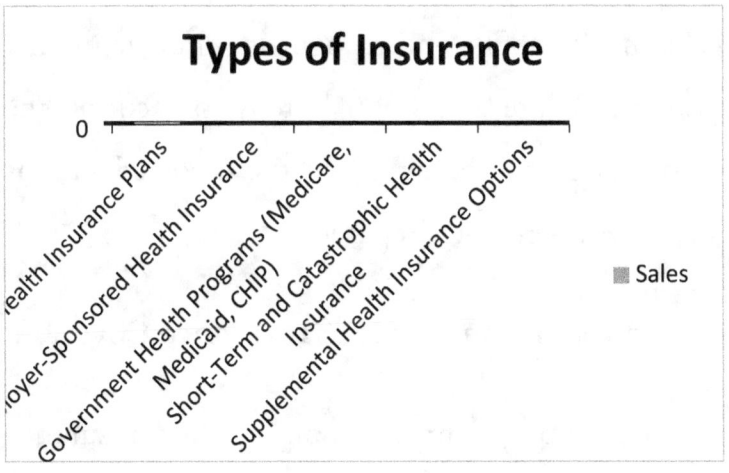

Fig.1

CHAPTER 4

ASSESSING YOUR INSURANCE NEEDS

Selecting the right insurance coverage is an important choice that directly affects both your financial security and your overall sense of well-being. Determining how much coverage you need, understanding your health insurance requirements, balancing cost with benefits, and recognizing life events that may alter your needs are all essential steps to securing the right protection. Here, we break down these considerations to help you feel confident and prepared.

4.1 Determining the Amount of Life Insurance Coverage

Determining the appropriate amount of life insurance coverage requires looking closely at your current financial obligations, future goals, and the needs of those who depend on you. Life insurance is not only about securing an income replacement ones will be taken care of in times of need.

1. **Calculate Your Financial Obligations**: Start by listing current debts such as mortgages, car loans, and credit card balances. Include any outstanding loans that would need to be paid off in your absence. These obligations ensure that your family is not burdened with sudden financial stress.

2. **Consider Future Expenses**: Include estimated costs for significant future expenses such as children's education, weddings, or even long-term care for aging parents. Factoring in these costs adds a layer of financial security for your family.

3. **Income Replacement**: Think about how long your loved ones might need income support. If you're the primary earner, your coverage should replace your income for a number of years to maintain their standard of living. A common guideline is to aim for 5-10 times your annual salary.

4. **Emergency and End-of-Life Costs**: Include the potential cost of medical bills, funeral expenses, and other end-of-life considerations. The goal is to ensure that your family won't face additional burdens during an already challenging time.

When calculating these amounts, use tools such as online insurance calculators or consult with financial advisors to arrive at a comprehensive figure. The aim is to strike a balance between realistic coverage and affordability, securing peace of mind without straining your current budget.

4.2 Evaluating Health Insurance Coverage Requirements

Health insurance is crucial for protecting both your health and financial security, ensuring access to necessary care without overwhelming costs. Understanding your current and future healthcare needs helps in choosing the best coverage for you and your family.

1. **Assess Your Health Status**: Start by considering your personal and family medical history. If you or your dependents have chronic conditions or a history of specific illnesses, opt for plans that cover regular treatments, specialists, and necessary medications.

2. **Routine vs. Emergency Needs**: Evaluate whether your coverage includes routine check-ups, preventive services, and emergency visits. Plans that provide comprehensive

preventive care can help catch health issues early and reduce overall long-term costs.

3. **Coverage for Dependents**: If you have a spouse or children who rely on your health insurance, ensure the policy provides suitable options for pediatric care, maternity benefits, and other specific services.

4. **Out-of-Pocket Costs**: Understand the financial impact of premiums, co-pays, deductibles, and maximum out-of-pocket expenses. It's essential to find a balance where you're protected against high medical bills without paying excessively high premiums. High-deductible health plans (HDHPs) paired with Health Savings Accounts (HSAs) can be useful if you're generally healthy and want lower monthly costs with the option to save for future medical expenses.

Review the summary of benefits provided by insurance companies, and don't hesitate to ask questions about coverage details. The better your understanding, the more prepared you'll be to make informed choices that align with your health needs and financial goals.

4.3 Balancing Cost and Coverage

Balancing the cost of insurance with the level of coverage you need is an ongoing challenge. Overpaying for extensive coverage you might not use can strain your finances, while underestimating your needs could lead to gaps in protection during critical moments.

1. **Prioritize Essential Coverage**: Identify what types of coverage are absolutely necessary. For health insurance, ensure coverage for emergencies and major illnesses comes first. For life insurance, focus on ensuring enough to replace your income and cover significant debts.

2. **Compare Different Plans**: Don't settle for the first plan you come across. Take the time to compare policies from multiple insurers, looking at premiums, deductibles, co-pays, and the provider network. A plan with a higher premium might offer more extensive benefits and lower out-of-pocket costs, which could be more cost-effective in the long run.

3. **Consider Supplemental Coverage**: Sometimes, basic plans may leave certain gaps that can be filled with supplemental policies such as critical illness insurance or accident insurance. These additions can offer financial

relief in specific circumstances without significantly increasing monthly premiums.

4. **Review Annual Changes**: Insurance needs can shift as life evolves. Reviewing your policies annually and comparing new options can help ensure you're not overpaying or missing out on new benefits.

Finding the right balance means not only focusing on cost but considering the protection and comfort it provides. Investing the time to regularly assess and adjust your coverage can save money and prevent future hardship.

4.4 Life Events That Affect Insurance Needs

Life is full of changes, and certain events can dramatically alter your insurance requirements. Staying aware of how these moments impact your coverage ensures you're never caught unprepared.

1. **Marriage or Divorce**: Getting married often means combining two sets of insurance needs. Updating your policies to reflect joint coverage for health, life, and home insurance can lead to savings and comprehensive protection. Conversely, a divorce typically requires separating policies and reassessing individual needs.

2. **Birth of a Child**: Welcoming a new child into your family changes your financial landscape. Ensuring you have adequate life insurance to provide for their future is vital. Similarly, updating health insurance to include pediatric services and preventive care is a must.

3. **Buying a Home**: Purchasing a home brings new responsibilities and additional expenses. Ensuring that your life insurance policy can cover the mortgage in the event of an unexpected death helps secure your family's home. Homeowners insurance also plays a critical role in protecting your investment.

4. **Career Changes**: A new job may come with different employer-sponsored benefits or require you to seek your own health insurance coverage if you become self-employed. Review the options carefully to understand the extent of new coverage and whether additional supplemental policies are necessary.

5. **Retirement**: Shifting from an active working life to retirement often means transitioning to different health insurance options, such as Medicare. Evaluating whether you need supplemental coverage to cover gaps not included in Medicare can make a significant difference in

maintaining good health without financial stress. For life insurance, consider whether you still need high levels of coverage or if a reduced amount suits your needs as your financial obligations lessen.

6. **Health Changes**: A sudden diagnosis or the onset of a chronic condition can dramatically shift your health insurance needs. Reevaluating your plan to ensure it accommodates frequent doctor visits, medications, or specialized care can provide peace of mind and reduce the impact of unexpected medical expenses.

These pivotal moments require thoughtful reassessment of your policies to ensure they align with your new reality. Taking the time to regularly check and adjust your insurance ensures that you remain protected as life changes.

By understanding and addressing your insurance needs, you take proactive steps towards protecting your financial future and supporting your loved ones. Whether reviewing life insurance coverage, evaluating health policies, balancing cost and coverage, or staying aware of life events that affect your needs, thoughtful planning leads to stronger financial security and lasting peace of mind.

CHAPTER 5

UNDERSTANDING POLICY DETAILS

Taking the time to understand the specifics of an insurance policy can make a significant difference in choosing the right plan and avoiding unexpected financial surprises. Many people find themselves frustrated by the fine print and complex terms, but by breaking down the main components, you can approach your decision with clarity and confidence.

5.1 Premiums, Deductibles, and Copayments

When selecting an insurance policy, premiums, deductibles, and copayments are the most commonly encountered terms. Each of these plays a vital role in defining your financial responsibilities and the overall cost of your coverage.

Premiums: The premium is the amount you pay periodically (monthly, quarterly, or annually) to keep your insurance policy active. The amount varies based on factors such as the type of insurance, coverage level, age, and health status. While it can be tempting to choose a policy with the lowest premium, it's essential to weigh the cost against the benefits provided. A low premium might come with higher deductibles and out-of-pocket expenses.

Deductibles: The deductible is the amount you must pay out-of-pocket before your insurance begins to cover specific expenses. For instance, if your health insurance policy has a $1,000 deductible, you will need to pay that amount for qualifying medical services before your insurance starts contributing. Policies with higher deductibles often have lower premiums, making them suitable for those who are generally healthy and do not anticipate frequent doctor visits. However, if you have ongoing medical needs, a lower deductible could be more beneficial, despite the higher premium.

Copayments (Copays): A copayment is a predetermined, fixed amount that you pay out-of-pocket for certain medical services or prescriptions at the time they are provided. For instance, your health insurance plan

might require a $30 copay for each visit to the doctor. Copays help manage immediate expenses, making services more affordable on a visit-by-visit basis. However, frequent copayments can add up, so understanding how they fit into the overall policy structure is crucial.

Balancing these three components involves considering your current health, income, and the likelihood of medical expenses. It's not just about picking what looks cheapest on paper but understanding what fits your lifestyle and needs without stretching your finances.

5.2 Exclusions and Limitations in Policies

Insurance policies often come with exclusions and limitations that define what is not covered under the plan. Knowing these can prevent unwelcome surprises when filing a claim.

Common Exclusions: Many health insurance plans exclude certain services such as cosmetic surgery, alternative therapies, and non-prescription drugs. Some policies also exclude pre-existing conditions, which can be challenging for those with ongoing health issues. Understanding these exclusions before committing to a plan is crucial to ensure it meets your needs.

Limitations on Coverage: Policies may have limits on how much they will pay for particular services or during specific timeframes. For instance, there could be a cap on how many physical therapy sessions are covered annually or a maximum amount payable for certain surgeries. If you anticipate needing these services, knowing these limitations helps you prepare or consider supplemental insurance options.

Waiting Periods: Some policies include waiting periods for specific types of coverage, such as maternity benefits or coverage for pre-existing conditions. This means you may have to wait a certain period after your policy starts before you can claim benefits for those services.

The key to navigating exclusions and limitations lies in thoroughly reading policy documents and asking questions. Feel free to contact your insurance provider or a trusted expert for clear guidance and answers to your questions. The better you understand what is excluded, the more prepared you will be to manage your healthcare expenses.

5.3 Riders and Additional Coverage Options

Riders are optional additions to your insurance policy that offer extra benefits or modify the terms of coverage. They can be essential for customizing a policy to meet specific needs and provide more comprehensive protection.

Types of Common Riders:

1. **Accidental Death Benefit Rider:** This rider provides an additional payout if the insured dies due to an accident. This extra financial support can help loved ones manage unexpected expenses or maintain their standard of living.

2. **Critical Illness Rider:** If the insured is diagnosed with a severe illness such as cancer, heart disease, or a stroke, a critical illness rider can provide a lump-sum payment. This financial cushion helps cover medical expenses, lost income, or any other financial burden during treatment.

3. **Waiver of Premium Rider:** If the policyholder becomes disabled and can no longer work, this rider allows the insurance company to waive premium payments while maintaining active coverage. This option can be invaluable during periods of financial strain.

4. **Term Conversion Rider:** For those with term life insurance, this rider enables the policyholder to convert a term policy into a permanent one without undergoing a new medical exam. It provides flexibility for individuals whose long-term insurance needs change over time.

5. **The Importance of Riders:** Riders enhance your insurance policy by offering added benefits and customization options tailored to your specific needs. While they come at an additional cost, the protection they provide can be well worth it, especially if your circumstances or future goals align with the added benefits. When considering riders, evaluate the potential cost against the risk and financial relief they offer.

5.4 Renewal and Policy Terms Explained

Understanding how and when your insurance policy renews is crucial to maintaining continuous coverage and avoiding lapses. Different policies come with various renewal terms, and knowing what to expect helps in making proactive adjustments.

Automatic Renewal: Many insurance policies renew automatically at the end of their term, ensuring you don't experience a lapse in coverage. While this can be convenient, it's important to review your policy at renewal time to determine if any changes in coverage or premium rates have occurred. Renewal periods provide a valuable chance to evaluate your current coverage and update your policy to align with your evolving needs.

Policy Term Lengths: The duration of a policy term can vary. Some policies last for a year, while others might cover longer or shorter periods. Short-term policies might offer lower premiums but can require frequent renewals and may not provide the same level of benefits as longer-term plans.

Adjustments During Renewal: Insurers may change terms, increase premiums, or modify coverage at the time of renewal. Reviewing the updated terms and comparing them with other options is essential to ensure you're still getting value for your money.

Grace Periods: Many policies include a grace period after a missed payment, allowing the policyholder to make a late payment without losing coverage. The length of the grace period varies by insurer but is typically between 30 to 60 days. Understanding this timeframe can prevent unintentional policy cancellations.

Reevaluating Your Needs: Policy renewal is a time to reflect on any changes in your life that may affect your coverage requirements. Life events such as a change in employment, a new medical condition, or significant financial shifts may require adjustments to your policy. This is an ideal time to review whether additional riders or modifications are necessary to keep your coverage aligned with your current situation.

Understanding these policy details provides clarity and empowers you to make choices that best serve your needs. Insurance is not just about paying premiums; it's about feeling confident that you and your loved ones are protected. Whether reviewing costs, examining exclusions, adding riders, or keeping up with renewals, staying informed helps ensure your insurance works for you, not against you.

CHAPTER 6

HANDLING THE APPLICATION PROCESS

Applying for insurance can feel overwhelming, especially with the abundance of forms, procedures, and potential for confusion. However, understanding the process step-by-step can turn this daunting task into a manageable one. Below, we break down how to approach life insurance, health insurance enrollment, medical underwriting, and common mistakes to avoid to help you make informed decisions with confidence.

6.1 How to Apply for Life Insurance

Taking out a life insurance policy is a meaningful way to protect the financial well-being of your loved ones and ensure their future stability. The process can be straightforward when approached methodically.

1. Assess Your Needs: Before starting your application, reflect on how much coverage you need. Consider your income, outstanding debts, future financial obligations like education costs, and the needs of your dependents. This initial step helps ensure you select a policy that truly meets your family's requirements.

2. Choose the Right Type of Policy: Decide whether a term life policy, which offers coverage for a specific number of years, or a permanent life policy, which lasts a lifetime, aligns best with your goals. Term policies tend to be more affordable, while permanent ones provide lifelong coverage and a cash value component.

3. Gather Necessary Documents: Most insurance providers require certain documents during the application process. These often include proof of identity (such as a driver's license or passport), financial records, and potentially past medical records.

4. Complete the Application: The application form itself will ask for detailed personal information—name, address, occupation, and lifestyle habits such as smoking or alcohol use. Be honest and thorough when answering these questions, as inaccuracies can affect your coverage or cause issues when making a claim.

5. Schedule a Medical Exam (if necessary): Many life insurance policies require a medical exam. This allows the insurer to evaluate your overall health and set an appropriate premium rate. The exam usually involves fundamental assessments like checking blood pressure, conducting blood and urine tests, and measuring height and weight.

6. Wait for Approval: After submitting the application and completing the medical exam, the underwriting process begins. The insurer reviews your application and medical information to assess risk and determine premium rates. This step can take a few days to several weeks.

7. Finalize the Policy: Once your application is approved, you will receive a policy offer. Review the terms carefully to ensure everything aligns with your expectations before signing and paying your first premium.

6.2 Health Insurance Enrollment Steps

Enrolling in health insurance can seem complex, but breaking it down into clear steps simplifies the process.

1. Understand Enrollment Periods: Most health insurance plans have specific enrollment windows. Missing these windows can mean waiting until the next open enrollment period unless you qualify for a special enrollment period due to life events like marriage, birth, or job loss.

2. Compare Available Plans: Before choosing a plan, evaluate the options available to you. This might include employer-sponsored plans, marketplace plans, or government programs like Medicaid and Medicare. Compare premiums, deductibles, out-of-pocket maximums, and covered services to select the plan that best suits your needs.

3. Gather Your Information: Have necessary documents ready, such as proof of income, social security numbers for all applicants, and citizenship documentation. If applying for government assistance, income verification documents like tax returns or pay stubs are essential.

4. Complete the Application: Applications can be completed online, over the phone, or on paper. Answer all questions accurately, including personal and financial information.

5. Provide Supporting Documents: Some applications may require additional documentation to verify eligibility, such as proof of address or income.

6. Choose a Plan and Pay Your Premium: Once approved, select your plan and make the first payment to activate your coverage. Ensure you pay within the specified timeframe to avoid delays.

6.3 Understanding Medical Underwriting

Medical underwriting is a process used by insurance companies to evaluate an applicant's health status and determine the level of risk they pose. Understanding how this step works can help set realistic expectations during the application.

1. Why It Matters: Underwriting helps insurers decide if they will offer you coverage and at what premium rate. For applicants, this can mean higher premiums or coverage limitations if significant health risks are identified.

2. The Medical Exam: This is a common part of underwriting for life and some health insurance policies. The exam usually includes measuring your blood pressure, recording your height and weight, drawing blood, and collecting a urine sample. The results provide the insurer with data on cholesterol, blood sugar levels, and other potential health markers.

3. Medical History Review: Underwriters will review your medical history, sometimes reaching out to your healthcare providers for further details. This really helps them to build a comprehensive picture of your health.

4. Additional Questions: Be prepared to answer questions about your lifestyle and family medical history. Conditions like diabetes or heart disease within your family can influence the insurer's assessment.

5. Outcomes: The underwriting process may result in standard approval, approval with a higher premium, or, in some cases, denial of coverage. If denied, seeking coverage from specialized providers or policies that don't require underwriting (like guaranteed-issue life insurance) could be options.

6.4 Common Application Pitfalls to Avoid

Despite thorough preparation, applicants often make common mistakes during the process. Being aware of these pitfalls can save time and avoid complications.

1. Providing Inaccurate Information: Omitting details or misrepresenting your health history can lead to denied claims or even policy cancellation. Always be truthful when filling out forms and answering questions.

2. Missing Deadlines: Whether applying for health insurance during open enrollment or responding to a life insurance offer, missing deadlines can mean losing coverage opportunities. Schedule reminders to stay on top of key dates and deadlines.

3. Overlooking Policy Details: Failing to read the fine print of your policy can result in misunderstandings about what is covered and what is excluded. Take the time to read through your policy and ask questions if anything is unclear.

4. Skipping the Medical Exam: While it may be tempting to opt for no-exam policies, these often come with higher premiums or limited coverage. If possible, complete the medical exam to improve your chances of obtaining better rates.

5. Not Comparing Plans: Settling on the first insurance plan you find without comparing options can lead to higher costs and inadequate coverage. Research multiple providers and plan options to find the best fit for your needs.

6. Ignoring Renewal Requirements: Some policies need to be renewed periodically. Failing to complete renewal paperwork on time can lead to a lapse in coverage. Always mark your calendar with renewal dates to avoid interruptions.

By following these steps and being aware of potential obstacles, you can approach the insurance application process with more confidence and ensure that you are taking the necessary measures to protect your financial and personal well-being. Thoughtful preparation, honesty, and attention to detail make all the difference in securing the right insurance coverage for you and your loved ones.

CHAPTER 7

MANAGING YOUR POLICY

Once you have an insurance policy in place, the task doesn't end there. Properly managing your policy ensures that you maintain the right level of coverage, stay aware of your responsibilities, and are prepared if you need to make a claim. Here, we provide guidance on keeping your policy current, understanding portability, making adjustments for life changes, and successfully filing claims.

7.1 Keeping Your Policy Up to Date

Keeping an insurance policy current requires more than just paying premiums on time. It's about actively reviewing and updating your policy to match your ongoing needs.

1. Regular Reviews: Life is constantly changing, and so are your coverage needs. Schedule a review of your policy at least once a year to ensure that it still meets your requirements. This simple act can highlight gaps in coverage or unnecessary components you may no longer need, helping you avoid overpaying for insurance that doesn't serve your current situation.

2. Contact Information: Keep your contact details up to date with your insurer. If your phone number, address, or email changes, it's essential to inform your insurance provider right away. Outdated contact information can lead to missed communication, which may impact important notifications or policy renewals.

3. Payment Methods: Double-check that your payment methods are current. A declined payment due to an expired card or an outdated bank account could lead to a lapse in coverage. Setting up automatic payments can help ensure that premiums are consistently paid on time, preventing accidental lapses.

4. Beneficiary Updates: If your policy includes beneficiaries, make sure to review and update them regularly. Life events like marriage, divorce, or the birth of a child may prompt a need to change your beneficiaries. Keeping this information current avoids conflicts or complications during a claim.

5. Document Storage: Maintain a safe and accessible place for storing policy documents, both physical and digital. These documents should be readily available in case you need to reference them or provide them when making a claim.

7.2 Policy Portability and Transfers

There may come a time when you need to transfer or take your policy with you, especially when changing jobs or relocating. Understanding how policy portability works helps prevent coverage interruptions and provides peace of mind.

1. Employer-Sponsored Health Plans: If you have health insurance through an employer and are changing jobs, you may be eligible for COBRA coverage, which allows you to temporarily continue your current health plan after leaving your job. Although this option often comes with higher premiums (since your employer no longer subsidizes the cost), it provides valuable coverage until you secure a new plan.

2. Life Insurance Transfers: Some life insurance policies are portable, meaning you can take them with you when you change employers. This is more common with supplemental or group life policies. Check the terms of your policy to see if portability is an option and understand any conditions that may apply, such as continued premium payments or adjustments to coverage.

3. Moving to a New State: If you relocate, especially across state lines, check with your insurer to confirm that your policy remains valid. State laws and regulations can affect insurance policies differently, so it's crucial to ensure your coverage adapts to the new location. In some cases, updating your policy may require new terms or even switching providers.

4. Transferring Ownership: If you need to transfer ownership of a life insurance policy to another individual or trust, this can be done through specific paperwork. Such transfers are often used for estate planning purposes and should be discussed with an insurance or legal professional to understand any tax implications.

7.3 Adjusting Your Policy for Life Changes

Life changes can dramatically alter your insurance needs. From new family members to career shifts, adjusting your policy helps ensure that your coverage continues to serve its purpose.

1. Marriage or Divorce: When you get married, consider updating both your life and health insurance policies. Adding your spouse as a beneficiary or dependent ensures they receive the appropriate benefits in the future. Conversely, after a divorce, make sure to update your policy to remove an ex-spouse as a beneficiary if that aligns with your wishes.

2. Birth or Adoption of a Child: The arrival of a new family member is a significant reason to update your life insurance policy. Adding a child as a beneficiary and increasing your coverage to account for future needs such as education expenses is a wise move. For health insurance, ensure that your policy covers pediatric services and wellness visits.

3. Career Changes: A new job or a shift to self-employment can affect the types of insurance you need. If your new employer offers health insurance, compare it to your previous policy to ensure it meets your needs. If you are transitioning to freelance work, you may need to purchase individual health and life insurance policies to maintain continuous coverage.

4. Home Purchase or Relocation: If you buy a home, updating your life insurance policy to cover mortgage costs ensures that your family is not financially burdened should anything happen to you. Additionally, moving to a new home or state may require adjustments to homeowners' insurance to reflect different risks and regulations.

5. Health Changes: A diagnosis or change in health status might prompt you to review your coverage. In some cases, it might make sense to add riders or adjust your coverage to ensure ongoing treatment costs are managed.

6. Retirement: As you approach retirement, your insurance needs shift. Reviewing your health insurance options, including Medicare and supplemental plans, is crucial to ensure continuous, affordable care. Life insurance may need to be adjusted or converted, as the primary goal changes from income replacement to legacy planning or estate coverage.

7.4 How to Make a Claim Successfully

Submitting a claim can feel overwhelming, particularly during challenging moments. Ensuring that you follow the right steps can make the process smoother and increase the chances of a successful outcome.

1. Review Your Policy First: Before filing a claim, read through your policy to understand what is covered and what documentation will be needed. This preparation helps prevent delays and ensures you have everything in order.

2. Gather Required Documentation: Claims often require various documents, such as proof of identity, policy details, medical records, and death certificates (for life insurance claims). For health insurance claims, include invoices, receipts, and any treatment notes from healthcare providers.

3. Contact Your Insurer Promptly: Notify your insurance company as soon as possible to begin the claim process. Some policies have strict timelines for when claims can be filed, so acting quickly is essential.

4. Follow Instructions Carefully: Every insurer has a set process for filing claims. Whether it involves completing forms online, mailing documents, or speaking to a claims adjuster, follow the steps as instructed. Missing details or skipping steps can delay the process.

5. Keep Communication Records: Document all communications with your insurer, including phone calls, emails, and any written correspondence. Keeping these records provides a clear trail should any disputes or questions arise during the claim process.

6. Be Patient but Proactive: While waiting for a claim decision can be stressful, most insurers aim to process claims efficiently. However, if you feel there has been an unreasonable delay, reach out to your insurer for updates feel free to ask questions or seek clarifications whenever necessary.

7. Appealing a Denied Claim: A claim denial doesn't have to be the final word. Many insurers allow for an appeal process. Review the reasons for the denial, provide additional supporting documents if necessary, and submit your appeal within the given timeframe.

Managing an insurance policy effectively means staying proactive and adapting to life's changes. Keeping your policy current, understanding portability, adjusting for significant life events, and being prepared to file claims all contribute to maintaining the protection you need. This thoughtful approach ensures you're not only covered but confident in the security that your insurance provides.

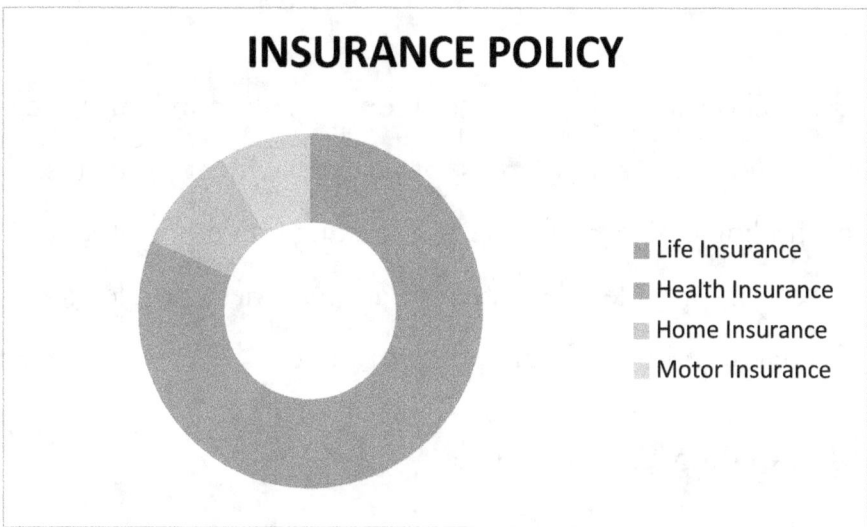

Fig. 2

CHAPTER 8

SOLVING COMMON INSURANCE PROBLEMS

This section offers practical solutions to common issues such as claim denials, policy lapses, premium payment problems, and finding coverage despite pre-existing conditions. Each subsection provides clear steps to address these problems effectively and help ensure peace of mind.

8.1 Handling Claim Denials

Receiving a denial for an insurance claim can be frustrating and disheartening, especially during a time when assistance is needed the most. However, understanding why a claim is denied and taking the right steps can turn the situation around. Here's how to approach it:

1. **Examine the Denial Letter:** Begin by thoroughly reviewing the denial letter to understand the specific

reasons your claim was rejected. Insurance companies typically outline the reasons for denial, whether due to incomplete information, policy exclusions, or errors in filing. Pinpointing the exact reason for the denial is key to deciding your next steps.

2. **Verify Your Policy Coverage**: Double-check your insurance policy to confirm whether the claim should be covered. Review the terms, conditions, and any specified limitations carefully. It's essential to have a thorough understanding of your policy to challenge any discrepancies.

3. **Gather Supporting Documents**: Collect all relevant paperwork, including medical records, accident reports, or communications that support your claim. Comprehensive documentation can strengthen your case.

4. **Contact the Insurance Company**: Reach out to the claims department to seek clarification and potentially provide any additional information they might need. Be polite but firm and maintain records of all communications.

5. **Submit an Appeal**: Most insurance companies have an appeals process for denied claims. Ensure you follow the appeal guidelines precisely, including submission deadlines and necessary forms.

6. **Seek Assistance if Necessary**: If the appeal is denied, consider reaching out to an insurance advocate or an attorney who specializes in insurance claims. They can offer professional guidance and may improve your chances of reversing the decision.

8.2 Dealing with Policy Lapses

A lapsed insurance policy can lead to a lack of coverage when it is needed the most, but there are ways to manage this issue effectively:

1. **Understand the Reason for Lapse**: Determine why the policy lapsed. Common reasons include missed payments, oversight during renewal, or changes in policy terms that were overlooked. Understanding the cause not only aids in resolving the current issue but also helps you take proactive measures to avoid similar problems in the future.

2. **Act Promptly**: Time is critical when dealing with a policy lapse. Contact your insurance provider as soon as you realize the lapse has occurred. Some providers offer a

grace period during which the policy can be reinstated without penalty.

3. **Inquire About Reinstatement**: Ask your insurance company if the policy can be reinstated and what conditions apply. You may need to pay outstanding premiums and possibly a reinstatement fee.

4. **Provide Updated Information**: In some cases, the insurer may require updated information, such as health assessments or proof of vehicle safety, to reinstate a lapsed policy.

5. **Explore Alternative Options**: If reinstatement is not possible or feasible, start looking for a new policy as soon as possible. Compare different providers and terms to find a plan that suits your needs and minimizes gaps in coverage.

6. **Implement Preventive Measures**: Set up automatic payments, reminders, or calendar alerts to ensure future payments are made on time and renewals are managed without delay.

8.3 Resolving Premium Payment Issues

Difficulty in making premium payments can lead to policy cancellations and loss of coverage. Below is how to address these challenges:

1. **Review Payment Terms**: Start by understanding your payment schedule and any grace periods provided by your insurance policy. Knowing how long you have before coverage is affected can provide peace of mind and allow for planning.

2. **Contact Your Provider**: If you are experiencing financial difficulties, reach out to your insurance company immediately. Some companies offer temporary payment plans, deferment options, or adjusted billing schedules that can help you maintain your coverage. **Evaluate Policy Options**: Review your current policy to see if adjustments can be made. For instance, opting for a plan with a higher deductible can often reduce your monthly premium.

3. **Seek Assistance Programs**: Depending on the type of insurance, there may be state or federal assistance

programs that can help cover premium payments. Research applicable programs and eligibility criteria.

4. **Consider Policy Adjustments**: If your financial situation has changed significantly, it may be wise to adjust your coverage to better align with your current budget. This could mean lowering certain coverage limits or dropping non-essential add-ons temporarily.

5. **Set up Alerts and Reminders**: To avoid future payment issues, establish alerts for upcoming due dates and consider setting up automatic payments.

8.4 Finding Affordable Coverage with Pre-Existing Conditions

Obtaining insurance coverage when you have pre-existing conditions can be particularly challenging, but it is not impossible. The following steps can help you navigate this process and find suitable options:

1. **Research Specialized Providers**: Look for insurance companies that specialize in high-risk coverage or have experience working with clients who have pre-existing conditions. These providers are often more flexible in their underwriting criteria.

2. **Compare Multiple Policies**: Use online comparison tools or consult with an independent insurance broker to explore different plans and pricing. Brokers can often find policies tailored to your specific health needs.

3. **Understand State Regulations**: Depending on where you live, state laws may provide protections that require insurers to cover certain pre-existing conditions. Take the time to understand these regulations thoroughly so you can make well-informed decisions.

4. **Consider Group Insurance Plans**: Group policies, such as those offered through employers or professional associations, may be more accommodating and less expensive. Such plans typically provide coverage without excluding pre-existing conditions

5. **Provide Comprehensive Health Information**: While it may seem counterintuitive, being transparent about your medical history can help insurers assess your application more favorably. This transparency can lead to customized plans that better meet your needs.

6. **Explore Public Health Options**: Depending on your situation, government programs like Medicaid or the Affordable Care Act (ACA) marketplaces might offer

affordable plans that cover pre-existing conditions without excessive premiums.

7. **Ask about Riders or Endorsements**: Some insurers may allow riders that specifically address pre-existing conditions. While this may add to the cost, it ensures your coverage includes what you need.

8. **Focus on Preventive Care**: Some plans emphasize preventive measures and wellness programs that help manage conditions without high out-of-pocket costs. These programs can provide valuable long-term benefits.

Finally, following these practical strategies, navigating insurance-related challenges can become less daunting. Whether addressing denied claims, dealing with policy lapses, resolving payment issues, or finding coverage despite pre-existing conditions, taking proactive steps will empower you to secure the insurance protection you need.

CHAPTER 9

HOW TO SELECT THE BEST INSURANCE PROVIDER

Finding the right insurance provider can seem overwhelming, with countless companies offering a variety of policies, making the right decision is essential for your peace of mind and financial security. This section provides practical tips on comparing insurance providers, understanding reviews and ratings, knowing what questions to ask, and recognizing signs of reliability in a provider.

9.1 Comparing Insurance Companies

When considering insurance providers, comparison is key. Each company has its strengths and weaknesses, and understanding these can make all the difference:

1. **Policy Offerings**: Start by evaluating the types of policies offered. Ensure the provider offers the coverage you

need—whether it's auto, health, life, or home insurance—with options that fit your specific requirements.

2. **Premium Costs**: Compare the premiums among different companies, but don't make price the only factor. A cheaper policy might lack essential benefits or come with hidden fees. Source for a balance that will meet affordability and comprehensive coverage.

3. **Coverage Limits**: Check the coverage limits in detail. Higher limits provide better protection but often come with higher premiums. Ensure you're comfortable with the coverage amount provided.

4. **Add-Ons and Flexibility**: Consider whether the insurer offers additional options such as riders or endorsements to tailor your policy. Having the ability to customize your coverage can provide significant benefits.

5. **Discounts Available**: Investigate potential discounts, such as for bundling policies or maintaining a good driving record. These can lead to considerable savings.

6. **Ease of Access**: Evaluate the company's user experience, including their website, mobile app, and customer support services. A seamless online platform or a helpful support team can make managing your policy much simpler.

9.2 Reading Reviews and Understanding Ratings

Customer feedback is an invaluable resource when deciding on an insurance provider. While no company is immune to negative reviews, understanding how to interpret these insights is crucial:

1. **Review Patterns**: Read through both positive and negative reviews to identify common patterns. Repeated complaints about slow claims processing or poor customer service can be red flags.

2. **Third-Party Ratings**: Check ratings from reputable third-party organizations like A.M. Best, Moody's, or Standard & Poor's. These ratings assess the financial stability of insurance providers, indicating their ability to meet policyholder obligations.

3. **Customer Satisfaction Surveys**: Look at surveys conducted by independent agencies such as J.D. Power. These often provide a broad overview of customer experiences across various aspects of the service, including claims processing and overall satisfaction.

4. **Context Matters**: Keep in mind that some negative reviews can be due to misunderstandings or isolated

incidents. It's important to read reviews with an objective mindset and focus on the bigger picture.

5. **Direct Testimonials**: If possible, talk to friends, family, or colleagues who have experience with the provider. Personal experiences can provide candid insights that go beyond written reviews.

6. **Response to Feedback**: How a company responds to feedback can be telling. Companies that actively address and resolve issues demonstrate a commitment to customer care.

9.3 Questions to Ask Your Insurance Agent

Speaking directly with an insurance agent is an opportunity to clarify doubts and understand policy details. Here are important questions to ask:

What Does My Policy Cover and Exclude: Make sure you fully understand what your policy includes and excludes.

1. This question helps prevent surprises during claim time.

2. **How Are Claims Processed?**: Ask about the process, timeline, and any potential issues that could arise during claims handling. This insight can help you

assess whether the company's claims process is efficient.

3. **What Are My Payment Options?**: Find out if the company offers flexible payment plans, automatic payment setups, or grace periods for late payments.

4. **What Discounts Am I Eligible For?**: Get detailed information on the types of discounts they offer and whether you qualify for them.

5. **Are There Any Additional Fees?**: Clarify whether there are extra costs for processing or policy changes. Knowing this up front can save you from unexpected expenses.

6. **What Is the Company's Financial Rating?** Confirm the financial standing of the company as a way to verify its reliability.

7. **Is There an Option to Bundle Policies?** Bundling can often lead to significant discounts, so asking about this option can be beneficial.

8. **What Happens If I Need to Cancel My Policy?** Understanding the cancellation process, including any penalties or refunds, is important for flexibility.

9.4 Signs of a Reliable Insurance Provider

Identifying a dependable insurance company requires observing certain key traits that indicate trustworthiness and competence:

1. **Financial Strength**: A reliable provider has strong financial backing, demonstrated by high ratings from agencies like A.M. Best and Standard & Poor's. This indicates the company's capacity to pay claims even in tough times.

2. **Transparent Communication**: A trustworthy company is transparent about its terms, conditions, and any fine print. Policies should be clear without ambiguous language.

3. **Responsive Customer Service**: How a company treats its customers says a lot about its reliability. A provider that offers prompt, helpful, and respectful service—both online and offline—is usually dependable.

4. **Claims Processing Efficiency**: Reliable insurers have a streamlined, efficient claims process and are known for paying claims promptly. Check for reviews and reports on claims processing times.

5. **History and Reputation**: A provider with decades of proven experience and a solid reputation in the industry tends to be more dependable than newer, unproven companies.

6. **Accessibility**: Reliable insurers provide easy access to policy management tools. Whether it's through a user-friendly website or a well-rated app, convenience in managing your policy is a positive sign.

7. **Strong Consumer Protection**: Companies that actively protect consumers' interests, such as offering fair dispute resolutions and having a transparent complaints process, stand out.

8. **Industry Recognition**: Awards and recognitions from industry groups can indicate that a company goes above and beyond in terms of customer service, innovative products, or ethical practices.

Remember, the goal is not just to find a provider that fits your budget but one that supports you when you need it most.

CHAPTER 10

MAXIMIZING YOUR INSURANCE BENEFITS

10.1 Leveraging Preventative Care Services

Maximizing your insurance benefits often starts with utilizing the preventative care services it provides. These services are designed not only to address potential health concerns early but to save on future, more significant medical expenses. Understanding how to use these services can lead to better long-term health outcomes and reduced out-of-pocket costs.

Preventative care typically includes a variety of screenings, vaccinations, and wellness visits. Many insurance plans cover these services without requiring you to pay additional fees such as co-pays or deductibles. This means that routine checkups and standard screenings for blood pressure, cholesterol levels, and certain types of cancer can often be scheduled without financial worry. Utilizing these benefits proactively ensures that potential health issues are detected early, when they are typically more manageable and less costly to treat.

It's essential to be aware of the specific preventative services your insurance policy covers. Begin by reviewing your policy documentation or consulting with your insurance provider directly. Ask questions like, Which routine screenings are included? or Are there age or frequency limitations on certain tests? Taking this step helps you avoid surprise expenses and provides peace of mind when arranging essential health appointments.

Aside from general checkups, preventative services include immunizations that help protect against diseases such as influenza, hepatitis, and pneumonia. By keeping up to date with these vaccines, you not only safeguard your own health but also contribute to the wider public health effort by reducing the spread of preventable diseases.

Insurance plans may also cover lifestyle-focused preventative measures, such as counseling for weight management, smoking cessation, and stress reduction programs. These services are invaluable for maintaining overall health and can significantly improve quality of life. For instance, seeking guidance from a registered dietitian through a covered counseling session can help you adopt healthier eating habits, potentially warding off chronic conditions like diabetes or heart disease.

It's worth noting that many preventative services are age-specific or recommended at particular life stages. For example, women's health services, including mammograms and pap smears, are often fully covered when done on a recommended schedule. Similarly, men's health screenings, such as prostate exams, are covered under certain criteria. Keeping track of when you are due for these essential checkups is critical.

Digital tools, such as apps or online portals provided by your insurance company, can help remind you when to schedule appointments and keep track of past visits. By taking the initiative to use these tools, you create a seamless experience that ensures you don't miss out on valuable health services that come at no additional cost.

Maximizing preventative care also involves understanding the potential limits within your plan. For example, while an annual physical may be covered, additional visits outside of this for other issues may not be unless specified. Understanding these details allows you to plan for potential costs and avoid unexpected bills.

Taking advantage of preventative care services is more than just a smart financial move; it empowers you to take control of your health, identify issues early, and develop a proactive approach to well-being.

10.2 Understanding Health Savings Accounts (HSAs) and Flexible Spending Accounts (FSAs)

Another key aspect of maximizing your insurance benefits is fully understanding and utilizing Health Savings Accounts (HSAs) and Flexible Spending Accounts (FSAs). These financial tools offer unique advantages that can help you manage healthcare expenses more effectively.

Health Savings Accounts (HSAs) is a special tax-advantaged accounts which is available to individuals are enrolled in high-deductible health plans (HDHPs). Contributions to HSAs are made pre-tax, which can reduce your taxable income and provide an immediate financial benefit. Additionally, funds in an HSA roll over year to year, meaning you won't lose unused money at the end of the year—a significant difference from FSAs.

To maximize the use of an HSA, start by contributing enough to take full advantage of any employer matching if available. This essentially gives you free money to help cover medical costs. HSAs are highly versatile and can be used to pay for qualified medical expenses, including prescriptions, doctor's visits, and even some over-the-counter medications. Beyond immediate expenses, HSAs can serve as a long-term savings strategy since funds can be invested and grow tax-free. This makes them a valuable tool for future medical costs, particularly in retirement.

When using HSA funds, it is essential to keep track of all receipts and documentation related to your medical expenses. This helps ensure that if you ever need to justify your withdrawals, you have the necessary proof on hand. Some financial institutions offer user-friendly apps and online tools to manage HSA spending, making it easier to keep a clear record.

HSAs come with contribution limits, which are updated yearly by the IRS. For 2024, the limit for individual coverage is $4,150, and for family coverage, it is $8,300. Understanding these limits and planning your contributions accordingly can help you maximize the tax benefits without exceeding allowed amounts.

Flexible Spending Accounts (FSAs) offer another tax-advantaged way to save for healthcare expenses, though they come with different rules and limitations. Unlike HSAs, FSAs are not tied to having a high-deductible health plan and are typically available through employer-provided insurance. The major downside to FSAs is the "use it or lose it" rule, which means that any funds not used by the end of the plan year may be forfeited. Some plans may allow a grace period or a limited rollover amount, but it's crucial to know your specific plan details.

Despite this limitation, FSAs can be a strategic way to set aside pre-tax money for predictable medical expenses, such as regular prescriptions or planned medical procedures. Estimating your annual healthcare needs and contributing an appropriate amount can help you avoid losing funds. Using your FSA for everyday eligible items like bandages, contact lenses, and other approved over-the-counter supplies is a smart way to utilize these funds throughout the year.

Both HSAs and FSAs allow you to pay for a wide range of healthcare-related expenses that might not be covered by your main insurance plan. This can include dental care, vision services, and specific therapies. Becoming familiar with what qualifies for reimbursement and keeping an organized system of receipts and records will make using these accounts simpler and more efficient.

To further maximize your benefits, consider using an FSA for short-term expenses while allowing your HSA to grow over time. This strategy can provide a balance of immediate and future financial support for healthcare costs.

Planning for Future Needs: One often-overlooked aspect of HSAs is their use in retirement planning. Since funds roll over year to year, an HSA can be a powerful asset if contributions are consistently made and invested wisely. Withdrawals for non-medical expenses after age 65 are allowed without penalty, though they are taxed as income. This gives an HSA a dual purpose—as a savings account for medical expenses and a backup retirement fund.

Using HSAs and FSAs Together: While you cannot contribute to both an HSA and a standard healthcare FSA simultaneously, some employers offer a "limited-purpose" FSA, which covers expenses like dental and vision. This type of FSA can be paired with an HSA, allowing for even more tax-saving opportunities.

10.3 Using Life Insurance for Estate Planning

Life insurance is not just a protective measure for your loved ones; it can also play an important role in estate planning. By using life insurance strategically, you can help ensure that your family members are financially secure after your passing, minimize tax burdens, and maintain control over how your assets are distributed.

One of the primary benefits of life insurance in estate planning is the ability to provide liquidity. When someone passes away, the estate often includes assets like property, investments, or business holdings that may not be easily converted to cash. The payout from a life insurance policy can help cover immediate expenses such as funeral costs, outstanding debts, and estate taxes without requiring your heirs to sell valuable assets.

To make the most of life insurance in your estate plan, it's important to assess your financial situation and determine the coverage amount needed to meet your family's future expenses. This involves considering your current debts, estimated estate taxes, and any ongoing financial support your dependents might need. Consulting with a financial advisor or an estate planning attorney can provide tailored advice to suit your specific circumstances.

There are different types of life insurance policies, such as term life insurance, which offers coverage for a specified period, and permanent life insurance, which remains in force for the time of your life as much as premiums are paid. Permanent policies often come with a cash value component that can be borrowed against or even used as an emergency fund during your lifetime. This added flexibility makes permanent life insurance attractive for those looking to integrate life insurance into a comprehensive financial strategy.

For individuals with substantial estates, setting up an Irrevocable Life Insurance Trust (ILIT) may be a wise move.

An ILIT holds your life insurance policy outside of your taxable estate, ensuring that the death benefit is not subject to estate taxes. This can preserve more of your assets for your beneficiaries while potentially reducing tax liabilities.

Naming Beneficiaries Wisely: Another crucial step in leveraging life insurance for estate planning is choosing the right beneficiaries. Naming your estate as the beneficiary might lead to the death benefit being subjected to probate, delaying the distribution process and potentially incurring additional costs.

CHAPTER 11

LEGAL AND REGULATORY CONSIDERATIONS

11.1 Insurance Regulations

Understanding the legal framework that governs insurance is essential for both policyholders and providers. Insurance regulations are in place to ensure fairness, transparency, and protection for all parties involved. These regulations vary by country and even by state, which can complicate the landscape for consumers.

In the United States, insurance oversight largely falls under state governments. Each state has its own insurance department responsible for overseeing the practices of insurance companies, monitoring compliance, and addressing consumer complaints. This regulatory oversight ensures that insurers operate in a manner that is fair and ethical, protecting consumers from predatory practices and ensuring the financial stability of insurance providers.

Key regulations include rules on rate-setting, which prevent insurers from charging excessively high premiums without justification, and mandates that ensure coverage for essential services. For instance, state regulations often require insurers to provide minimum levels of coverage, ensuring that policyholders have a baseline level of protection. Additionally, insurers must meet solvency standards to prove that they can pay out claims, which protects consumers from the risk of an insurer going bankrupt.

Being aware of these regulations can help consumers make more informed decisions when selecting an insurance provider. It's advisable to check with your state's insurance department for any specific rules that may impact your policy and rights as a policyholder.

11.2 Consumer Rights and Protections

Understanding your rights as a policyholder is essential for guaranteeing fair and equitable treatment. Consumer rights and protections in insurance are designed to prevent discrimination, ensure transparency, and offer mechanisms for resolving disputes.

A fundamental right afforded to consumers is the privilege of being well-informed. Insurers are legally obligated to provide clear and comprehensive information regarding policies, including coverage details, exclusions, and the terms and conditions. This ensures that you understand what you are signing up for and can avoid unpleasant surprises when filing a claim.

An essential right is the ability to appeal if your claim is denied. If your insurance company denies a claim, you are entitled to know why and to challenge that decision if you believe it is incorrect. Many states require insurers to provide a written explanation for claim denials, which gives you the opportunity to review their reasoning and take appropriate action.

Additionally, consumers have the right to privacy. Insurance companies gather sensitive personal and financial details to evaluate risk and offer appropriate coverage. In the United States, regulations like the Health Insurance Portability and Accountability Act (HIPAA) play a crucial role in safeguarding this information also ensure that your private health information is safeguarded and utilized solely in accordance with your given consent. Protections are also in place to guard against discriminatory practices. Insurers cannot deny coverage or charge higher premiums based on certain protected characteristics such as race, gender, or pre-existing conditions. These protections help ensure that insurance services are accessible and fair for all consumers.

11.3 The Affordable Care Act (ACA) and Its Influence on Healthcare

The Affordable Care Act (ACA), introduced in 2010, transformed the health insurance system in the United States, ushering in substantial reforms and reshaping access to healthcare for millions of Americans. The ACA's primary objective was to broaden access to affordable healthcare coverage while enhancing the quality of care provided. One of the most notable impacts of the ACA is the requirement for insurance companies to cover individuals with pre-existing conditions. Prior to the ACA, many people found it difficult or impossible to obtain coverage if they had a history of chronic illness or other health issues. This change has allowed millions of Americans to access necessary healthcare without facing exorbitant premiums.

The ACA also implemented subsidies to assist low-income individuals and families in affording health insurance coverage. These subsidies are based on income and household size and can significantly reduce monthly premium costs for those who qualify. The Affordable Care Act (ACA) also introduced health insurance marketplaces, designed to simplify the process for consumers to compare various plans and select one that aligns with their needs and financial capacity.

Preventative services were another focus of the ACA. The law mandates that certain preventative services, such as vaccinations and screenings, be covered without cost-sharing. This measure encourages early detection and treatment of potential health issues, which can lead to better outcomes and lower overall healthcare expenses.

The ACA also placed limits on how much insurers can spend on administrative costs and profits. Known as the medical loss ratio (MLR) rule, this regulation requires insurers to spend at least 80% of premium revenue on medical claims and healthcare improvements. If an insurer fails to meet this requirement, they must issue rebates to policyholders, which promotes fairness and transparency.

Despite its benefits, the ACA has faced criticism and legal challenges, particularly regarding the individual mandate that required most Americans to have health insurance or face a penalty. While this mandate was effectively repealed in 2019, the ACA's core provisions remain intact, continuing to shape the healthcare system and insurance market.

11.4 Legal Recourse for Disputed Claims

Dealing with denied insurance claims can be a stressful and frustrating experience. However, knowing that there are legal avenues for recourse can provide some peace of mind. If you find yourself in a situation where an insurance claim is denied, there are several steps you can take to challenge that decision.

The initial step involves thoroughly examining the denial letter. Insurance companies are required to provide a detailed explanation of why a claim was denied. Understanding the reason behind the denial will help you determine if there was a misunderstanding, an error, or if the denial was justified according to your policy's terms.

If you believe a denial was issued in error, you have the right to submit an appeal. Most insurers have an internal appeals process where you can submit additional documentation or request a review of the decision. This process often requires you to act within a specific timeframe, so it's essential to move quickly.

If the internal appeal does not resolve the issue, you may be eligible to pursue an external review. An external review involves an independent third party that assesses your claim and the insurer's decision. If the external reviewer concludes that the denial was unwarranted, the insurance company is required to reverse their decision and process the claim. In cases where disputes cannot be resolved through appeals, legal action may be necessary. Policyholders can take their case to court, particularly if they believe the insurer has acted in bad faith. Bad faith claims can arise when an insurer fails to investigate a claim properly, unnecessarily delays payment, or denies a claim without a valid reason. Consulting with an attorney who specializes in insurance law can provide guidance on how to proceed.

State insurance departments can also be a valuable resource. They often have consumer assistance programs to help guide you through the appeals process or mediate disputes between you and your insurance company.

Being aware of your rights and the steps you can take when disputes arise helps empower you as a policyholder. With the right knowledge and preparation, you can handle claim denials confidently and pursue the benefits you are entitled to.

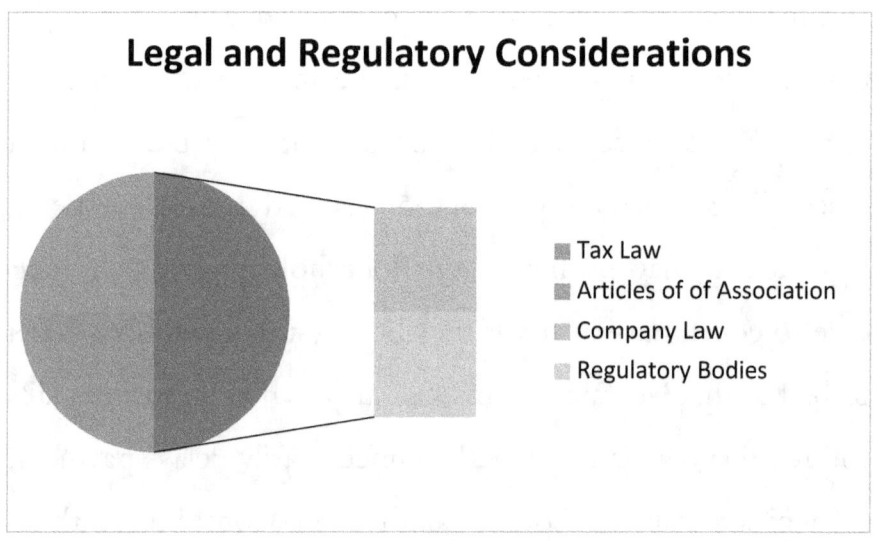

Fig. 3

CHAPTER 12

INSURANCE AND FINANCIAL PLANNING

12.1 Integrating Life Insurance in Your Financial Plan

Life insurance is often viewed purely as a safety net for loved ones, but it can be an integral part of a well-rounded financial plan. When used strategically, life insurance provides financial stability and supports long-term goals. The primary purpose of life insurance is to ensure that your dependents are financially secure in the event of your passing. However, its benefits go beyond basic coverage.

One way life insurance can be integrated into your financial plan is through policies that include a cash value component, such as whole life or universal life insurance. These policies accumulate cash value over time, which can be accessed for loans or withdrawals to cover major expenses such as college tuition or emergency medical bills. This built-in savings mechanism provides a level of financial flexibility that term life insurance does not offer.

Life insurance can also act as a vehicle for wealth transfer. By naming beneficiaries, you can ensure that the death benefit is distributed according to your wishes, bypassing probate and avoiding potential delays and fees associated with the probate process. This feature is particularly useful in estate planning, allowing for an efficient transfer of wealth to heirs.

For those seeking a more robust financial strategy, an Irrevocable Life Insurance Trust (ILIT) can be established. This trust holds your life insurance policy outside of your taxable estate, preserving the full death benefit for your beneficiaries while reducing estate tax liability. Integrating life insurance in this way not only provides peace of mind but can also strengthen your overall financial security.

12.2 Health Insurance as Part of Financial Security

Health insurance plays a pivotal role in protecting against significant financial risk. Without it, a serious illness or unexpected accident can lead to overwhelming medical bills that can destabilize even the most carefully managed finances. By incorporating health insurance into your financial plan, you create a buffer that helps safeguard your savings and long-term investments.

The right health insurance policy ensures that routine medical expenses and unexpected healthcare costs are manageable. When choosing a plan, consider factors such as premiums, deductibles, out-of-pocket maximums, and coverage networks. A plan with a higher premium and lower deductible might be more suitable if you have ongoing medical needs, while a lower-premium, higher-deductible plan may work well for those in good health who need coverage primarily for emergencies.

In addition to providing coverage for direct healthcare costs, health insurance often comes with access to wellness programs and preventative services that support overall well-being. By staying proactive with your health through regular checkups and screenings, you can potentially avoid larger medical expenses down the road. This approach helps maintain not only your health but also your financial stability.

Incorporating health insurance into your financial strategy requires budgeting for monthly premiums and potential out-of-pocket costs. It's important to review your policy annually and adjust your plan as needed based on changes in your health, income, or family size. This ensures that your health insurance continues to support your financial security without straining your budget.

12.3 Budgeting for Premiums and Costs

Effective budgeting for insurance premiums and related costs is essential to maintaining financial health. Insurance can represent a significant portion of your monthly expenses, so integrating it into your budget requires careful planning.

Start by reviewing your overall income and determining how much you can allocate towards insurance without compromising other essential expenses. This may involve prioritizing different types of coverage based on your current stage of life. For example, life insurance might be a higher priority if you have dependents, while comprehensive health insurance is crucial for protecting against unforeseen medical bills.

It's also wise to set aside funds for out-of-pocket costs such as co-pays, deductibles, and any services not covered by your plan. Creating a dedicated savings account for these expenses can prevent financial strain when medical or insurance-related costs arise unexpectedly.

When budgeting for insurance premiums, take advantage of discounts that may be available through your employer or for bundling different types of insurance policies. For instance, combining home and auto insurance with the same provider can often lead to reduced rates. Reviewing your policies annually to check for potential savings opportunities or more cost-effective plans is a proactive way to keep your insurance budget balanced.

Lastly, it's important to consider inflation and the rising cost of medical care when planning your budget. Adjusting your budget periodically and accounting for these changes ensures that you are adequately prepared for future expenses.

12.4 Building a Long-Term Insurance Strategy

Developing a long-term insurance strategy is essential for sustaining financial health and protecting against unforeseen life events. This strategy involves assessing your current coverage, projecting future needs, and making adjustments as your life circumstances change.

Begin by evaluating your existing insurance policies and identifying any gaps in coverage. This can include life, health, disability, and property insurance. For instance, if you only have basic health insurance, you might want to consider supplemental coverage that provides additional financial support for critical illnesses or long-term care.

A solid long-term insurance strategy should also involve periodic reviews to adapt to new life stages. Major life changes such as marriage, having children, buying a home, or approaching retirement can significantly alter your insurance needs. For example, new parents may need to increase their life insurance coverage to provide greater financial protection for their family, while individuals nearing retirement might focus on long-term care insurance to manage potential healthcare needs as they age.

Diversifying your insurance portfolio can also add layers of protection. Disability insurance, for example, is often overlooked but can be invaluable if an illness or injury prevents you from working for an extended period. This type of policy ensures that you continue to receive income, preserving your financial stability during difficult times.

Finally, a well-rounded insurance strategy includes an emergency fund specifically for insurance-related costs not covered by your existing policies. This can include high deductibles, uncovered services, or any premium adjustments. Setting aside a portion of your savings for these scenarios ensures that your financial plan remains strong even when unexpected events occur.

Building a long-term insurance strategy requires regular review, proactive adjustments, and a comprehensive understanding of your financial goals. By doing so, you can create a plan that offers peace of mind and supports your financial well-being over time.

CHAPTER 13

INSURANCE TRENDS AND FUTURE OUTLOOK

13.1 Current Trends in the Insurance Industry

The insurance industry continuously evolves to address the shifting needs of consumers while adapting to economic changes and regulatory developments. One of the most notable trends in recent years is the increased focus on personalized insurance plans. Insurers are leveraging data analytics and consumer feedback to offer more tailored policies that meet individual needs, from flexible premium structures to customizable coverage options.

Sustainability is also becoming a major trend in the insurance world. Companies are recognizing the importance of environmental, social, and governance (ESG) criteria and incorporating them into their business practices. This shift reflects a broader societal push toward responsible and ethical business practices and appeals to policyholders who prioritize these values.

Another significant advancement is the emergence of on-demand insurance. This model allows consumers to purchase temporary or usage-based coverage through digital platforms. For instance, someone renting a car for a short period can secure coverage for just that timeframe. This type of flexible coverage aligns with modern lifestyles, especially for younger consumers who prefer minimal long-term commitments.

13.2 Innovations in Life and Health Insurance

Innovations in life and health insurance are reshaping how policies are structured and delivered. One significant advancement is the incorporation of wellness programs into health insurance plans. These programs encourage policyholders to maintain healthier lifestyles by offering incentives such as reduced premiums or cash rewards for meeting certain health goals. Insurers are increasingly partnering with tech companies to integrate wearable devices and apps that track physical activity, sleep, and other health metrics.

In the realm of life insurance, accelerated underwriting processes are becoming more prevalent. Traditional life insurance often involved lengthy underwriting periods that required extensive medical examinations and background checks. Now, advancements in data analysis and digital tools allow for quicker assessments, enabling applicants to receive approval in days rather than weeks.

Telehealth services, once considered supplementary, have become integral to many health insurance plans. These services provide a convenient way for individuals to consult with medical professionals, reducing the need for in-person visits and enabling faster care. Telehealth has proven particularly valuable during global health crises, demonstrating its potential to remain a permanent fixture in health insurance plans.

13.3 The Role of Technology in Insurance

Technology is playing an increasingly pivotal role in the insurance industry, influencing everything from customer service to claim processing. Artificial intelligence (AI) is at the forefront of this shift, providing tools that enhance risk assessment, fraud detection, and customer experience. Insurers use AI-driven algorithms to analyze massive data sets, making more accurate predictions about policyholder behavior and risk profiles.

Mobile applications and online portals have transformed how consumers interact with their insurance providers. Policyholders can effortlessly manage their accounts, submit claims, and access policy details directly from their smartphones with just a few taps. This convenience has raised consumer expectations, pushing insurers to continue enhancing their digital offerings.

Blockchain technology is another innovative force impacting the insurance sector. It promises greater transparency and security by allowing data to be stored in a decentralized manner, reducing the risk of data breaches and fraud. Smart contracts, which use blockchain technology, can automate claims processes, ensuring that policyholders receive payouts quickly and efficiently.

Machine learning and predictive analytics are also being employed to customize policies and enhance customer retention. By analyzing customer data, insurers can identify trends and adjust policies to better suit individual needs. This capability not only improves customer satisfaction but also helps companies remain competitive in a rapidly changing market.

13.4 Preparing for Future Insurance Needs

As the insurance landscape continues to evolve, preparing for future needs involves staying informed about emerging trends and adapting coverage as necessary. Consumers should be proactive in understanding how technological advancements and market shifts might impact their current and future policies.

One strategy for preparing for future insurance needs is to keep an eye on new products and services offered by insurers. For example, climate change is influencing the creation of new types of insurance that cover risks associated with extreme weather events. Homeowners in areas prone to natural disasters may need to look for policies that include comprehensive coverage for climate-related damages.

Long-term care insurance is another area to consider as part of future planning. With an aging population, the demand for policies that cover the costs of extended medical and personal care is expected to grow. Consumers should evaluate options that align with their anticipated needs as they age, balancing premiums with potential benefits.

Maintaining flexibility is also key to navigating future insurance needs. Policies that offer adjustable coverage levels or options for riders can provide added protection as circumstances change. For instance, adding a critical illness rider to a life insurance policy can provide financial assistance if the policyholder is diagnosed with a serious condition.

Finally, it's important to stay educated on regulatory changes that may impact coverage. New laws or amendments to existing regulations can alter the structure and availability of certain types of insurance. By staying informed and consulting with insurance professionals as needed, consumers can ensure that their coverage evolves alongside industry advancements and personal needs.

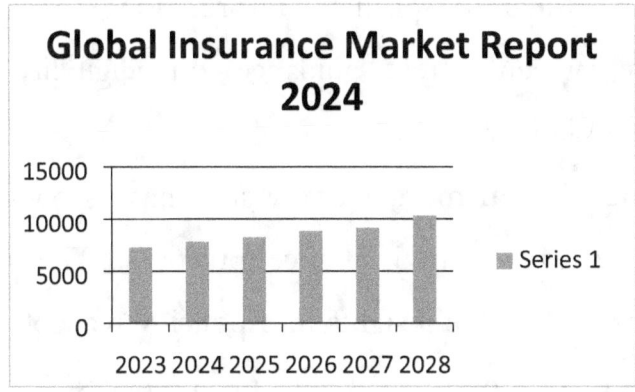

Fit 4

CHAPTER 14

RESOURCES AND SUPPORT

14.1 Trusted Sources for Insurance Information

When seeking information about life and health insurance, it's essential to rely on credible and accurate sources. Here are some reliable options:

- **Official Government Websites:** Government portals such as **HealthCare.gov** provide detailed insights into health insurance options, including the Affordable Care Act (ACA), enrollment timelines, and other coverage options. For Medicare-specific information, visit **Medicare.gov**, which offers guidance on eligibility, benefits, and enrollment.

- **State Insurance Departments:** Every state has its own regulatory body overseeing insurance practices. These departments offer valuable insights into policies available within the state. For example, California residents can utilize the **California Department of Insurance** for localized guidance. A comprehensive directory of state insurance departments can be found through the

National Association of Insurance Commissioners (NAIC) website.

- **Consumer Advocacy Groups:** Organizations like **Consumer Reports** and the **NAIC** provide impartial reviews and guidance, helping individuals make informed insurance decisions.

- **Educational and Research Institutions:** Institutions like the **Kaiser Family Foundation** regularly publish research and analysis on health policy, making their findings a trusted resource for understanding complex insurance topics.

14.2 Tools to Compare Insurance Policies

Finding the right policy involves careful comparison to ensure it aligns with your needs and financial capacity. These resources are designed to simplify the process and improve overall efficiency.

- **Online Comparison Platforms:** Services like **Policygenius** and **NerdWallet** enable users to compare insurance quotes by entering personal details and preferences. These resources offer detailed, side-by-side evaluations of premiums, coverage options, and customer satisfaction ratings.

- **Insurance Calculators:** Tools such as the **Life Insurance Calculator** by MoneyGeek assist in determining the appropriate coverage amount based on your income, debts, and future financial goals.
- **Financial Strength Ratings:** Agencies like **AM Best** and **Standard & Poor's** evaluate insurance companies' financial stability, helping you assess their ability to meet claims obligations.
- **Customer Feedback and Surveys:** Platforms like **J.D. Power** provide satisfaction rankings and reviews that reflect real user experiences with insurance companies.

14.3 Key Contacts for Assistance

Accessing the right support can help resolve concerns and clarify doubts about insurance policies. Here are some important contacts:

- **Insurance Company Support Services:** Most insurers offer customer service lines to assist with policy details, claims, or general inquiries. For example, **Cigna** provides multiple channels for customer assistance.

- **State Health-Insurance Assistance Programs (SHIP):** State Health Insurance Assistance Programs (SHIPs) provide free, unbiased counseling to Medicare beneficiaries and their families, assisting them in making informed decisions about their healthcare coverage.
- **Centers for Medicare & Medicaid Services (CMS):** For Medicare or Medicaid-related queries, contact CMS at **1-800-MEDICARE (1-800-633-4227)** or visit **Medicare.gov**.
- **NAIC Helpline:** For general insurance-related concerns or to locate your state's insurance department, visit the **NAIC** website.

14.4 Key Insurance Terms to Know

Understanding the language of insurance can prevent misunderstandings and empower better decision-making. Below are some frequently used terms:

- **Premium:** The cost of your insurance policy, that you pay monthly or annually.
- **Deductible:** A deductible is the portion of expenses you are required to pay directly from your own pocket before your insurance coverage begins to contribute toward the costs.

- **Copayment (Copay):** A fixed amount you pay for healthcare services at the time of care.

- **Coinsurance:** Coinsurance is the part of the cost you have to pay, shown as a percentage, after you've paid your deductible. For example, with a coinsurance rate of 20%, you are responsible for paying 20% of the approved expenses, while your insurance provider covers the other 80%.

- **Beneficiary:** The beneficiary is the person or entity chosen to receive the benefits from a life insurance policy upon the policyholder's passing.

- **Policyholder:** The Actual owner of the insurance policy.

- **Underwriting:** The process insurers use to assess risk, determining your premium and eligibility for coverage.

- **Exclusion:** Specific conditions or situations that your insurance policy does not cover.

- **Rider:** A supplementary feature you can add to your policy, providing extra coverage or enhanced benefits.

- **Claim:** A formal request to your insurer for reimbursement or coverage of services or losses.

- **Network:** A group of healthcare providers and facilities contracted with an insurer to offer services at negotiated rates.

- **Out-of-Pocket Maximum:** The maximum amount you must pay during a policy year for covered services. After reaching this amount, your insurer covers all remaining costs for that year.

- **Grace Period:** The grace period is the timeframe following a payment due date during which you can pay your premium without your coverage being canceled.

- **Policy Term:** The period during which your policy is active. At the end of this term, you may need to renew your policy.

- **Pre-Existing Condition:** A health condition that existed before your policy's start date. Some policies may restrict coverage for these conditions.

- **Cash Value:** For certain types of life insurance, like whole life policies, this represents a savings component that accumulates over time and can be accessed by the policyholder.

CONCLUSION

Understanding and effectively using life and health insurance can make a meaningful difference in your financial and personal well-being. This guide was created to give you the tools and knowledge needed to make informed choices that protect you and those you cherish. With the right coverage, unexpected medical expenses and life events become manageable, turning moments of uncertainty into times of resilience.

Choosing the best insurance policies and using them wisely is not just about paperwork or premiums—it's about peace of mind and the assurance that you have taken proactive steps to safeguard your future. By considering your current and future needs, budgeting smartly, and staying informed about industry trends and regulations, you create a safety net that supports your long-term goals and provides comfort in times of need.

As life changes, so do your insurance needs. Reviewing your policies regularly and adjusting as necessary ensures that your coverage remains relevant and beneficial.

www.ingramcontent.com/pod-product-compliance
Lightning Source LLC
Chambersburg PA
CBHW071518220526
45472CB00003B/1070